Upstage Your Neighbors:
A Guide for Preparing Your Home to Sell

Patrick S. Tremblay

RATTLEDASH MEDIA, LLC

ISBN 978-0-557-48515-4

First Edition

Printed in the United States of America

This book is for the Home Stager

Upstage Your Neighbors:
A Guide for Preparing Your Home to Sell

By Patrick S. Tremblay

Tremblay House of Design, an Interior Design firm in Santa Clarita, CA, has 10 tips which his clients use to ensure their homes sell as quickly as possible and for the best market price. When the homeowner places their home on the market, these hints are effective whether they choose to stage the home themselves or hire a professional to expedite the task for them.

Tremblay House of Design has been operating in the Southern California and Northern Nevada since 1992.

Professional Staging Managers charge either a single consultation fee per hour (perhaps $100.00) or provide their services on a square foot basis. The average staging cost per room ($250.00) can increase with increased square footage. Materials fall under a different charge, and depend on the extent of the client's desired materials. As with any contracted work, it is best to get multiple quotes which itemize the services to be performed so that maximum value can be assured for an affordable price. As a word of caution, using a professional might be disturbing until realization sets in that their opinions and suggestions are directed toward preparing the most appealing product and not, as it might seem a bashing of the homeowner's decorative tastes or skills.

Whether the staging is being done by the homeowner or a professional, here are the 10 tips which can yield a timely and profitable sale. They are divided into 4 parts, making a good first impression, presenting each room well, removing clutter and cleaning, and attending to details while the home is being shown.

First things first . . .
Get off to a good impression.

1. Create a good first impression

Each home has only one opportunity to give a positive first impression, and that "curb appeal" must be created. Most importantly, the yard and house must look well cared for and appealing.

- All weeds and dead foliage should be removed from the front and back yards.
- The trees and bushes should be trimmed so they do not block walkways or windows.
- The grass should be fertilized, mowed and edged.
- If in season, some flowering plants might be added to the flower beds.
- The driveway, sidewalks, curbs and gutters should be scrubbed clean.
- Paint faded walls or trim in natural, earthy tones which compliment the neighborhood colors.
- If painting the house isn't an option, always paint and repair the garage and front doors.
- Put out a new welcome mat.
- Clean the exterior light fixture. Make sure it is working
- Be sure the house numbers are bright and visible to the public.

Secondly, after you enter the home, rooms should be presented for their function. For example, the dining room should be defined as a dining room, not as a utility room/office dining room. When buyers enter a room, it is important that they can visualize their own possessions in that space. Because the seller is also facing a move, Tremblay House of Design suggests that, as the seller prepares each room; all unnecessary items are boxed and stored in a rental unit.

NOTES

The goal of tips 2 through 6 is to make the home look attractive, comfortable, livable, and ready for the new owner to move in their furniture and belongings.

2. Make the entry and living room welcoming

Once past the clean front door, and having established a good first impression, the prospective buyers will be interested in viewing the remainder of the home.

- Remove extra jackets, shoes, and other items in the entry,
- Hang mirrors to add visual space to a small entry.
- Add a feeling of space to the living room by removing excess furniture and accessories so that buyers can mentally place their own furniture in the room; the goal is for the prospective buyer to key on the room rather than on critiquing the decorative choices.
- Arrange the room to direct attention to the room's main feature such as a picture window or fireplace.
- Minimize accessories (Tremblay recommends grouping one, three, or five items per space as "odd" numbers of items are more appealing than even) using them to enhance not dominate any space.

NOTES

3. Create a spotless kitchen

The home's heartbeat is found in the kitchen, so spend some extra time on this important room.

- Remove all pictures from the refrigerator.
- Clean refrigerator and food storage shelves to 1/3 of their maximum contents.
- Clear the counters, except for a small bouquet of flowers or a cookbook, to accentuate their extent and availability for electrical appliances.
- The stove and oven must be sparkling.

NOTES

4. Turn the master suite into a sanctuary

For many, the master suite is a retreat after a hectic day; the buyer will want to visualize their future here.

- Clear and clean all furniture surfaces.
- Refresh the linens.
- Add silk or live plants.
- Remove your personal photographs and items with any religious connection; the house is being sold, not the personality of the present owners.

NOTES

5. Present an exceptionally clean and fresh bathroom

The seller cannot afford to show any bathroom that is not bright and odor free.

- Repair all grout and caulking.
- Deal with mold & bacteria by sanitizing the toilet, sinks, shower and tub.
- Clean floors thoroughly, including behind toilets and under sinks.
- Clear out cabinets. Remove anything others should not see.
- Polish mirrors and fixtures (replace chipped mirrors)
- To make the bathroom interesting, add matching towels and fresh soap.

NOTES

6. Tidy all closets

Closet space is very important, and gives homebuyers the opportunity to gain an impression of how nice their belongings will look in a well kept closet.

- Rearrange closet contents so that clothes closets, for example, contain only clothes, not vacuums, ladders and food.
- Make sure closets are not overstuffed; pre-pack for the up-coming move and store all unneeded items.
- If excess items must stay in the closet, be sure it is in neatly stacked containers.
- Organize clothing and shoes by size and color.
- Pack and store out-of-season and seldom worn clothing.

NOTES

Tips 7 through 9 will create space and brighten the home.

7. Brighten the walls

Clean walls and woodwork are important in creating a good impression.

- Remove most wall hangings and pictures; remove picture hooks, fill hole (not toothpaste!) and spot paint for touch-up.
- If a wall or room needs fresh paint, paint using light, warm colors which are more appealing than bright colors.
- Wallpaper must be clean and in good repair; otherwise, it should be removed.

NOTES

8. Reduce clutter to a minimum

Although implied in many of these tips, it must be emphasized: clutter is deadly to a sale. Too many books, stacks of papers, and lots of knick-knacks are "clutter" as is oversized furniture and clutter detracts from the good qualities of the home.

Tremblay suggests critically studying photographs of each room to determine what contents are unnecessary so that they can be packed in boxes stored.

Make a priority list of the items to stage with, pack for the move, or discard/donate

NOTES

9. Thoroughly prepare the garage, back yard and pet kennel

A professional will emphasize the importance of a clean and tidy home. Don't overlook these following aspects.

- The garage will appear large and functional if the work bench is neatly arranged, loose items are stored in plastic bins, garden tools are hung on wall hooks, bicycles are stored off-site or hung from the ceiling between cars, and oil stains on the floor are removed. Pre-packing the garage and storing these boxes off-site is a good way increase the perception of useable space in a garage.
- The back yard should be pleasing as it is often used as a playground for youngsters and for entertaining guests. Keep bikes, tools, and yard toys out of view, or neatly 'parked'. If there are water features, be sure they are up to code, working, and clean – a non-working water feature screams "costly repair" to the prospective buyer.
- Because not all homeowners are pet owners, be sure no pet offends these important visitors. If possible, board all pets after the home is prepared for selling and especially at the times your home is being shown. If boarding is not possible, be sure to maintain a clean, healthy environment for the pet that is as far away as possible from the walk-through route, such as leaving a cat in the laundry room with a litter box, rather than allowing it the run-of-the-house. Your pet will show you gratitude as well.

NOTES

Finally to tip 10, those last minute details which can help secure the sale or, if not done, might turn off someone who was almost ready to make an offer.

10. Create an attractive overall environment

As the prospective buyers walk through the house, attention to this last list of fine points may help instill a positive overall impression.

- Wash windows and clean carpets before the first showing and vacuum regularly afterward.
- Clear and dust all furniture daily.
- Open window treatments each morning and leave all lights on for maximum brightness.
- Place a fresh floral arrangement or a small plant in a room or two.
- Add candles or fruit in a decorative bowl on the dining room table.
- Set the mood by playing soft instrumental music in the background.
- Wash dishes and empty trash daily.
- Leave a typed note which covers any concerns for the realtor, such as a pet in the laundry room.

In accomplishing all these tasks, it is imperative that; **1)** clutter be reduced to a minimum, **2)** all surfaces be kept as clear and clean as possible, and **3)** every space or focal accent be defined and displayed to its best advantage.

Potential buyers who can quickly see a home's positive features and can picture themselves living in each of the rooms are more likely to make a timely and more market-appropriate offer. Tremblay House of Design has applied this 10 step staging strategy, and knows by experience that clients can effectively prepare their homes, promote successful sales, and can "upstage their neighbors."

NOTES